MEN AND
COLLECTIONS

BRIAN JENNER

MEN AND COLLECTIONS

CONTENTS

COLLECTORS AND COLLECTING: SHOWING OFF WHAT YOU'VE GOT

In their own way collectors are striving for excellence. They want to have the biggest, the rarest, the most unusual, the oldest, the most expensive, the complete set. They want a collection which makes other people gasp, 'Wow, look at that!'

However, to choose collecting as a field of excellence is quite unusual. There is nothing more exciting for a little boy in shorts than to collect football cards, comics, stamps, cars or marbles. It is part of the miraculous process of discovering the world. But that process usually ends abruptly with Mum throwing it all in the bin one day when you're out.

If it doesn't end there it can take on a completely different form in adulthood. Adult males can bring to their habit discipline, compulsion and money. As one collector of cereal packet toys confesses, 'When I was a child I could never complete the sets. But now I can.'

Many collectors are on a mission to preserve something from the past: a postbox from a certain period, a railway sign from a long-abandoned station or simply a lovingly crafted matchbox. It can be a response to the experience of seeing something beautiful destroyed or a desire to recreate some powerful childhood emotion.

The collector can see himself as the 'custodian' of history. It may seem odd that a grown man might want to make lists, wrap things up in polythene or put them in alphabetical order. But if he has confrontation at work or chaos at home, isn't it quite natural to want to escape?

So why is it predominantly a male thing? Most likely it is a reflection of the male urge to hunt and the need to focus on one particular thing. Since women juggle tasks, they cannot understand these singular obsessions. Some men are not allowed to show off their collections. They are confined to the loft or the shed.

THE JOY OF SETS

Collecting combines two passions: a love of hoarding things and the search for the unattainable. The collector always has a story: 'The day I discovered such and such...' or 'My first oven'.

There are many social benefits to do with collecting. It allows men to get together, to understand each other, to appreciate beautiful things. Collectors love the history of their objects. A collection provides meaning, structure and purpose to life. You get a couple of examples and then you specialize. You then have a Holy Grail, which can be a particular football kit or a rare cactus.

Of course there are degrees. You know it's a problem when you partner leaves you, when you can't get in the spare room and when you consider spending hundreds of pounds on a beermat. A hobby is like one's relationship with money. It is good to be well-organised and take care of your investments. It is mad to hoard them and let them be an obstacle to relationships with others.

The urge to collect reveals an inability to let go. The names that are given to collectors – arenophiles, phillumenists, tegestologists – sound like psychiatric conditions. Collecting is a neurosis, but for some collectors, the more entrenched the neurosis the more proudly they can wear the badge. One collector says, 'An old German man once told me that you can only call yourself a collector after 15 to 20 years. It's a passion. We've been doing it for well over 30 years and we'll never sell any.'

Collectors struggle to deal with the disorder and complexity of the world by doing something positive and often unconventional. The men in this book have all retained that child-like passion for discovery and marvel. Some might think them mad, but they inhabit their own delightful worlds, oblivious to the opinions of others. The psychiatrist Thomas Szasz wrote, 'Life is potentially a big empty hole and there are few more satisfying ways of filling it than by striving for and achieving excellence.' Here's to excellence.

Brian Jenner

SWEET MEMORIES

It could be a surrealist installation, but in fact Stephen has created his own enchanted world, which he can reach by turning right before the bathroom. He has converted his spare bedroom into a 1950s grocery shop. He has put lino on the floor, posters and adverts on the wall, he has acquired a fine pair of scales and has hundreds of old fashioned packets: Rowntree's Fruit Gums, ancient Mars bars and bottles of fizzy pop (filled with coloured water).

'You can't eat the stuff, it's far too old,' says Stephen. The boxes of old washing powder, tea and coffee, and loaves of bread fascinate neighbours and friends. He fills the packets to make everything look authentic and has retail incentives, like the 'penny tray'. He even wears the overalls. The only thing that is missing from the illusion is a cash register. The rest of his house is entirely modern.

When Stephen isn't in his shop he's a 47-year-old man who works in plastics.

"It brings back memories of childhood."

DIESELS WOULDN'T BE ALLOWED

Laurie has 285 steam train plates in his house, which can be a problem. Laurie confesses, 'Several years ago, Queen Alexandra slipped from my hands, broke the picture rail and crashed through the bedroom floor.' Another fell down in the garage and stoved in his wife's car door.

Amongst his collection he has plates from India, Cuba and Spain and several from Russia. Twenty years ago a British naval attaché sent him two in a diplomatic bag wrapped in copies of Pravda. It started when he was working for a locomotive firm in Leeds. 'I love the romance of steam trains and I travel all over the world to look at them.' He has recently been to Eritrea, where they have re-introduced steam trains after the country's terrible war.

'I have to clean them six times a year. I spread it over a week or else my arm would fall off. I'd never sell them. They're like pets.'

"Every plate has its own story."

COLLECTING LIKE BARNACLES ON A SHIP

'I collect things for a purpose, I want to find out more about them,' says Frank, though he admits it is also a 'wonderful madness'.

After finding an English handmade gramophone in a friend's attic 30 years ago, Frank tried to find out more about it but couldn't get any information. So he acquired dozens of the things, and wrote and researched the book, 'The EMG Story', which tells how a London fish salesman, Ellis Michael Ginn, founded a company that made amazing gramophones.

The men who built them would not accept anything less than perfection. They went through different models from 1924 to 1934 and the results set Rolls Royce standards. Though not well-known in the UK, they are much prized in Japan. 'Sound reproduction hasn't moved on at all. There is no volume control, and when you listen it's like a real live performance,' says Frank, who plays his 78s, which only last three minutes.

"Unbelievable to listen to. Great in a power cut."

THEY'RE NOT BREAKABLE OR HEAVY

Gordon took a practical approach to getting a hobby. His voice wasn't strong, so he couldn't do amateur dramatics. He had asthma so didn't want anything that involved animals or bad weather. He only had limited space, so when he got his own house, beermats proved perfect. 'They give hours of pleasure, especially in winter time.'

Tegestologists, as they are called, have an annual convention where you can buy and sell your mats. Gordon is not much of a drinker but he will have a few beers to justify going into the pub.

Years ago someone contacted him to say that he had a treasure trove of beermats in his attic, which he was prepared to sell for a very small fee. Gordon, full of excitement, visited the man. They went into the attic, opened the ancient box and all the mats had crumbled. He now keeps his own collection in metal filing cabinets and only puts doubles on show.

16

"They're woodpulp – they could get woodworm."

BLOSSOMING AMONGST THE THORNS

Phil has been collecting cacti for 42 years. The first he acquired as a six-year-old. It started off the size of a golf ball; it is now the size of a football.

There seems to be a streak of masochism in Phil's passion because the ones he enjoys growing most are the *turbinicarpus*, which are really slow growing and difficult to keep. 'It's a way of relaxing. You do find yourself talking to them. The ones I have grown up with I've become emotionally attached to – like children.' The thrill of collecting for Phil lies not in acquiring more cacti, but in finding the rarer ones.

Some cacti can live for 100 years, so many of his 350 plants could outlive him. The Aztec Indians used one sort to grind into a powder and make a drug a bit like LSD. 'They're so rare I wouldn't dream of doing that,' protests Phil, and so far he has had no visits from the local constabulary.

"I like to feel they know me."

19

ALTER EGO

Graham is a retired lawyer. He has 7,000 items of Edward VIII memorabilia in a garage at the bottom of his garden. When asked what his family think of his hobby, he says they think he's 'quietly strange'.

It all started when he was given an Edward VIII Coronation teaplate by his wife. Here was a bizarre object: something commemorating an event that never happened.

Graham now hoards any piece of Edward he can get hold of – mugs, tins, toasting forks, magazines, postcards, banners... He charts everything to do with the disgraced monarch: his movements day by day, whom he had lunch with, what he was wearing. Whenever he sees something particularly expensive, he'll find it difficult to resist. Has he any regrets? Graham says that one of the neighbours has got a chamber pot with an Edward VIII insignia. 'They won't sell it to me, but they get no pleasure out of it,' he complains.

"It's an obsession, I admit."

21

A SICK HOBBY

'Collecting fulfils a whole range of psychological needs,' says Aidan, 'the excitement of the hunt, the joy of finding a rare one, the competition with other collectors and the escapism from real life.' Aidan should know – he started at 13, collecting airport paraphernalia. Living on a remote island, it brought exoticism into his life, but his mother ordered him to chuck the stuff out. So he started to specialize in airline sickness bags.

He has 1,300 different bags, but 3,000 if you include his 'swapsies'. It's not such a strange thing to collect – see www.sicksack.com, for example. Aidan's favourites are his Iraqi Airlines bag and one from Finland with a cartoon on it depicting a queasy reindeer.

However, his hobby is under threat. 'Plane journeys are becoming so smooth. The sickness bag could be on the way out. If ever we had a convention, this would be one of the worries we would discuss.'

"I've never had to use one."

TRANSPORTS OF DELIGHT

Andrew likes nothing better than to cycle over to the Continent on a Royal Mail bicycle and create mayhem. He's been over 62 times. 'I haven't got the postman's garb, but people still wave me down to give me their postcards and letters, thinking they'll get to their destination quicker. Most people are terribly surprised to see me cycle off the ferry.'

A lifelong enthusiast for classic commercial bikes, Andrew has 24 Royal Mail standard-issue bicycles. Many he has reconstructed meticulously from a mangled state. He cycles 4,000 miles a year.

In 1985, the Government banned the resale of mail bikes, so they're now impossible to get hold of. Many of them are sent to Africa on a charity scheme. But Andrew still manages to get hold of older ones from time to time. 'I am trying to keep a little piece of the jigsaw, and keep alive a tradition of the British commercial bicycle,' he says proudly.

"I am a perfectionist. I restore the bikes in perfect detail."

LIMITED COLLECTIONS

In 1999 Bob went on holiday to New England, USA. He was impressed by the atmosphere in the diners so he bought a book about them as a souvenir.

He discovered they started off in the 19th century as horse-drawn carriages for workers on newspapers. They were small businesses which were family run. The 'portable' nature of them reflected a particularly American way of doing business. Bob's son found the internet auction site, Ebay, and Bob realised he could collect models, books, videos and even a roadside magazine to do with diners.

The appeal of collecting was that there was only ever a small number of porcelain models, mugs and tins associated with diners. Bob could own them all. He explains, 'I put the PC on every morning before I go to work and check Ebay to see what items have been put on. I've never bought anything for more than $50.'

"My family think I'm mad. I think they're mad."

A LIGHT IN YOUR LIFE

Lorry driver, Ray, likes to show off his blowlamps. He's got 220.

'I exhibit them at shows and I get a lot of information from old plumbers. You glean a lot from other people – far more than from other sources.'

Blowlamps are things that people usually throw away, but Ray likes to preserve them. He's got one which was used in a World War II tank; others are interesting because you discover who made them and where they were made. Does he actually light them up and do anything creative with them? 'Not very often,' he says. 'The petrol ones are very dangerous – they could explode – but the paraffin ones aren't so bad.'

His collection has been banished to the shed, but his wife is tolerant of his hobby. 'She likes to come along to the shows. My sons travel the world and I get them to find a few as well.'

"I live in the country. I am always interested in old machinery."

FURRY ACQUAINTANCES

Guy has acquired 200 tarantulas over 15 years. He doesn't give them names. He feeds them once a month. He doesn't handle them. He doesn't really get attached to them or feel particularly depressed when they die. Yet he does feel he is on a mission to educate people about their good side. 'There's a lot of mis-information about spiders,' he says.

Guy has created an amazing website, www.giantspiders.com, which details species, shows short videos and offers suggestions on how to care for tarantulas (including essays on their elaborate mating procedures). There is also a forum, which provides information on everything from where to buy cheap fresh crickets (spiders' favourite dish) to a web link to the Russian Tarantula Society. Guy's brother was also keen on collecting creepy-crawlies: in his case it was butterflies and moths. You would think that his obsession would put off girlfriends, but apparently not.

"I'm not interested in other types of collections. It's got to be alive."

A CEREAL COLLECTOR

Nick is a 37-year-old bank manager with two children and a wife. He is also an obsessive collector of old cereal packets and the curious toys you find in them.

He explains the many pleasures that come with collecting: 'When I get them out they hold memories, and when I show friends they remember, too. I'm particularly fond of the Tom & Jerry toys brought out by Nabisco in the early '70s.' Nick writes for a collectors' magazine and builds his collection by attending boot and card fairs. The cereal companies also give him things. Some of his stuff goes back to 1900 and items like a Thunderbird vehicle can be worth as much as £100.

Do his children eat cereal? 'I keep pouring it down their throats – my five-year-old only gets the spare toys. He understands I collect them.'

"I couldn't complete the sets at the time."

IT'S ALL YOU NEED TO MOW

'Don't let the grass grow under your feet!' shouts the programme of the Lawnmower Museum. The museum is Brian's glowing tribute to the garden machinery industry, of which he is so fond.

Are you an obsessive collector? 'I suppose I would have to be,' says Brian. 'Lawnmowers are not the sexiest of subjects.' Like most collectors, Brian has a precise knowledge of his possessions. The earliest prototype appeared in 1799, although Edwin Budding is credited with inventing the lawnmower in 1830. The most recent are the 'robot' lawn mowers (battery- or solar-powered) dating from 1995.

It started when his father owned a DIY shop and would restore old 'mowers. Brian has formative memories of being given rides in the grass boxes. Aren't they dangerous? 'More people are injured by plant pots than lawnmowers,' he counters. His museum has over 200 different models, including one owned by Prince Charles. See www.lawnmowerworld.co.uk.

"Most lawnmower collectors tend to be in the closet."

THINGS BROUGHT BACK BY MISSIONARIES

Collecting barbaric things to display around the house appealed to Alan. The idea struck him while reading Oscar Wilde's 'Picture of Dorian Gray', which features a character who keeps tribal artefacts in the genteel Victorian interior of his home.

Like many collectors, Alan complains that his pastime costs a lot more than it used to. Do any of his masks have any sinister powers? 'Most of them are benign and serene. There is one particularly vicious looking one from the Congo. Some have some particularly gungy patterns on them, the figurines have nails in them and chicken blood.'

Alan is trying to build up a collection of masks from all over the world and he can identify the differences between Nigerian, West African, Indian and Alaskan ones. 'My wife tolerates them. What I love about them best is that my mother-in-law loathes them. It's worth having them up for that.'

36

**"Little kids love them –
I go 'Grrr!' down the stairs."**

ONE DAY ALL THIS COULD BE YOURS

The Matchbox Label Society that Peter belongs to is a select group. There are manual workers, accountants and even a multi-millionaire. However, the millionaire is a bit of a pain at auctions because he holds his hand up until he gets whatever he wants. This is a problem for Peter because he collects a particular type of matchbox label, and it is difficult to find something he hasn't got. Usually the millionaire gets it.

Peter began collecting when he was 12. He has about 3,000 – a manageable number because he can remember almost every one he's got. It interests him to locate the factory where each matchbox was made. 'Even though they were made to be thrown away, the Victorian and Edwardian ones were works of art.'

Another problem for the Matchbox Label Society is that most collectors are in their sixties, so there aren't the younger ones coming through. But Peter does his bit to keep the hobby alive through his website (www.matchbox-labels.co.uk).

"I don't collect numbers – that doesn't appeal."

TRAFFIC CONE MAN

David was narrowly beaten in a 'most boring husband' contest on a television show – just because he has developed a life-long interest in traffic cones. He has 500 cones, but the Guinness Book of Records only acknowledges 137. 'You need a sharper eye to spot the difference,' says David.

He started working on traffic cones when he was 17. He then set up a plastics company to make his own. A legal dispute meant that he had to prove he wasn't copying someone else's. And so began an obsession. Where does he store them? 'In the loft, the garage, the summerhouse, the woodshed, the childrens' bedrooms and on the mantelpiece,' he says. 'They stack well.'

David plays musical cones with his children at parties. 'They have to touch a cone when the music stops – and the prize is under the big cone.'

"People like cones. They have so many uses."

A SELF-CONFESSED DISNEY NUTCASE

Dave's wife had to wait nine years for a new kitchen, because her husband indulged his love of Disney. It's Dave's way of dealing with the hustle and bustle of the modern world. After a hard day in the office, he would go to his 'Disney' room and put on a video or some Disney music. 'It's a way of escaping reality. Everybody has a bit of Peter Pan in them, and I like to lose myself – going back to when I was six or seven.'

'Disney' Dave's favourite character is Happy, the dwarf. 'I am a bit like him, I always seem jolly and robust.' Having built up a haulage company over the years, Dave has now sold up and bought his own Disney shop. It means he now supplies his family of 1,600 Disney collectors with all the memorabilia they need. 'It's a lot cleaner and they pay up front,' he says.

Dave's children make their own contributions to his collection, grateful for a dad whose idea of heaven is to go to Disneyland, Disneyworld or Disneyland Paris. The only one they haven't visited (yet) is in Tokyo.

"I liked it so much, I bought the shop."

MILKING IT

Paul estimates that there are about 150 collectors of milk bottles and dairy-related items in the UK. As the editor of the quarterly magazine 'Milk Bottle News', he should know.

He is only 25 but he has already got 5,000 milk bottles. He stores them in his own shed and his parents' shed. He likes the different designs and the adverts they used to have on them. Now that the supermarkets sell milk in their plastic containers, the milkman and the milk bottle are on the way out.

After a spell working in a dairy, Paul says he wouldn't mind becoming a milkman himself. 'The dairies are fighting to get milkmen, because it's a six day week and you have to get up at two in the morning.'

He also has long service medals and replica milk vehicles which has meant spending quite a lot of money on his collection. 'My family think it's a bit strange,' says Paul.

"For me it's a second pension."

THE QUEST FOR THE MISSING KIT

When Neal was a small boy he got a full Liverpool kit for Christmas. It was his best present ever. Now at 33 he has 150 strips. 'I try not to be systematic. I like the lackadaisicalness of my hobby. The internet site Ebay has made it too easy. I only want the ones that are really rare. I like to go abroad to watch football and maybe swap with another fan.'

For Neal the kit has to have some significance – the kit Maradonna wore when he was at Napoli or the Milan kit that Ruud Gullit would have sported. 'I've been searching for the Admiral Wales kit 1976/7 all my life. I came close when I found the away strip, in a child's size.'

Neal thinks that football kits can be part of a common universal consciousness. 'Whenever I go out in one, somebody will come up to me and say, "Where did you get that from? I remember that." It's always a talking point.'

"I only really want the red one."

A SOLID SYMBOL IN CHANGING TIMES

Arthur's daughter is worried that collecting might be hereditary. Her dad collects post boxes. His motivation? 'I hate things being thrown away just because they are no longer modern.'

It all began when Arthur was on holiday and he found a wooden postbox in a skip. He renovated it, and people have been giving other postboxes to him ever since. He recently moved house which involved transporting his collection of 130. Thankfully he found a removal firm with experience of moving elephants.

Arthur seems to find the idea of post boxes rather poetic. 'They are linked up with our birthdays, marriages and deaths. They also have so many clues to our history. Did you know that Scottish post boxes have a different crown on them because they can't put Elizabeth II? Elizabeth I was not popular up there.'

Arthur is quite grateful for the fact that the boxes are no longer readily available. His daughter is too.

"My wife thinks it's a first class hobby."

HISTORY IN YOUR POCKET

'The psychology of the collector is like the psychology of a gambler,' says Yasha. 'There is a flow of adrenaline when someone has got something for you. There is the psychology of completion, when you have collected five different ones you want all of them. Then there is a wonderful fraternity of collectors. I ask people if they are collectors, and there is an immediate understanding.'

As Yasha ruminates on his precious cards, banknotes and maps, he reels off dates and assigns them with historical significance. He is holding an early 15th century Ming Dynasty banknote – both an early example of a currency and an early example of printing.

He expounds in the same way about playing cards, which in the French Revolution were also used as money because of a shortage of paper: 'If only my history teacher had used collecting to learn about history, I would have been a historian now.'

"Collectors are like Freemasons without the handshake."

ARMCHAIR GENERAL

By day Colin is a Senior Unix Systems Administrator (something in computers), but when he has finished work he makes the most of his collection of military vehicles.

He started by acquiring a few rucksacks and other militaria, and then took an interest in US vehicles dating back to the 1960s and the Vietnam War, (see his website at www.m151.info). One of his trucks has four machine guns on it, which might create some anxiety out on the roads, so he keeps them on a nearby farm and hires them out for James Bond films. Colin's father was in the Royal Engineers and Colin learnt to rebuild cars as a boy.

When people see him on the road, they like to stop and wave or cadge lifts with him. Does he drive them to the supermarket? 'I've taken one of them but it has a 21 metre turning circle, which doesn't work very well.' Is he planning to organise a military coup? 'They haven't annoyed me that much yet...'

"My wife hates it with a passion."

LIKE FATHER, LIKE SON

For Derek, collecting runs in the family. His father began the collection of AA badges and, after his father died, it was his mother who urged him to take it over. But Derek didn't limit himself to badges. Pride of place in his collection is an AA sentry box – an AA man had it in his garden for years, and, when he moved, he gave it Derek along with his uniform. Among the things Derek has hoarded there are oil pourers, transport-related china, petrol cans, Esso men...

Derek's wife is not a fanatic, but his mum is still keen at 88. The neighbours don't really get to see the collection because they have high hedges. What motivates Derek? 'I suppose we're custodians, keeping these things for the future.' Completing sets and holding on to a good investment also seem to be factors. As far as badges are concerned he wants to 'get every one'. He can now seek out his treasures on a trestle table on the other side of the world: Derek has a friend in Australia who takes photographs of things in 'Autojumbles' for him, so he can choose whether to buy them or not.

"We've all had a bit of collecting in us."

A TEETOTAL PUBCRAWL

For over 25 years, David, a retired schoolteacher and librarian, has written about the history of breweries. Six years ago he set out to photograph every pub in his county. It was a disciplined task. He used one film reel a month, but he didn't go out every day – it depended on the weather. He took over 800 in the end, and they are now filed in a big cardboard box.

His wife is a school inspector who travels the country, so David can always go along with her and snap a few pubs or visit the local record office. A sentimentalist at heart, he laments the modernization of public houses. 'Nearly always the appearance of pubs has been ruined by turning them into roadhouses or just one big room. It's sad.'

Another disappointment is that for the past 12 years David has had diabetes. So he hasn't actually been able to have a drink in any of the pubs he cherishes so much.

"In my day, pubs had two or four rooms."

KEEPING YOUR FEET ON THE GROUND

What's the appeal? 'Nostalgia, I suppose,' says Kevin, who owns 160 pairs of running trainers. However, Kevin isn't a conventional collector: 'All the trainers have to fit me. I'm not sentimental. If they wear out, they go in the bin.' How do people react when they see his collection? 'Wow! Look at that lot,' he says.

Trainers seem to be big. Pop star, Noel Gallagher has got a massive Adidas collection. Such is their value, Adidas contacted all their old stockists across Europe to find out if they still had some of their old shoes from the '70s and '80s.

Kevin, 34, has both feet firmly in the 'utilitarian' school of collecting. 'The shoes are for my own personal use. They seem to have built up over the years, I just see some and think, "Cor, that's a nice pair of shoes, I'll have them."' What does he look for in a trainer? 'Style and colour.'

"New shoes are never going to be like the old shoes."

UP THE SPOUT

It was in 1986 that Vince made a trip to Stoke-on-Trent to buy a kitchen. While he was there he saw two teapots displayed by the Price & Kensington Teapot Factory. He bought them. A few weeks later he went back to buy some more.

17 years later, Vince is the founder of the Totally Teapots Collectors Club – the webmaster and publisher of 'Let's Talk Teapots'. Every year now they have a convention in a nearby hotel, which includes a teapot auction. At the height of his collecting mania, Vince travelled 100,000 miles in three years to find teapots.

Vince has 1,500 himself, which adorn every shelf and ledge in his home. Miss Piggy, Mrs Thatcher, Ronald Reagan and HM Queen Elizabeth are among the teapot characters that peer down at him at the breakfast table. What does his wife think? 'She doesn't like it when it becomes obsessive – she'd sell half of them tomorrow if she had the chance. It's hard for a collector to part with them, even when he's got two the same.'

"It's bigger than people think."

ON THE RECORD

'They are spreading like a weird vinyl fungus across the living room,' confesses Fraser, sheepishly. A natural hoarder, he started collecting Marvel comics when he was three and bought his first LP when he was seven. He now has 10,000 weird and wonderful records.

'It's very compulsive. Every time I go out I get five or six I don't even want.' Fraser works as a fashion designer and listens to his records every day. 'I won't listen to a track all the way through, though.'

The collection is an investment and a talking point for visitors. Favourites include his selection of psychedelic children's LPs and one of an Indian doing covers of Michael Jackson in Hindi. Fortunately for his neighbours he's got a large, old house with thick walls. Fraser has a group of friends who have a similar addiction. 'We call ourselves "Vinyls Anonymous" and we're very open about how sad it is. Grown men sprinting after record boxes.'

"No CDs – that's the devil's work."

A WORLD AUTHORITY ON CHILDREN'S TOYS

Tim was fed up with children being unimpressed by his magic tricks. 'My big brother can do better than that,' they would say. And so he decided to specialize in toys instead.

Tim does research on toys from all over the world and entertains children at parties by showing them off. You can see him in a Chuck Hoberman Sphere, wearing a six-armed costume with hologram glasses. He's surrounded by the suitcases he uses to transport the toys. With 9,000 toys in his collection, his bedroom looks like a luggage shop and the house is gradually becoming overwhelmed. He rather dreads seeing a large toy which he can't resist.

The man in the house next door called him an 'interesting neighbour', which in the suburbs is quite an accolade. Tim has retired from his day job and he now travels to toy fairs in places like Nuremberg and New York. 'I'm not commercially minded, but the hobby keeps me alive and in touch,' says Tim.

"I love entertaining people."

A HAPPY COOKER

The urge to collect often seems to be rooted in a powerful childhood experience. For James, it was at the tender age of five, when he saw a grand stove being disposed of after it had been condemned by the Gas Board. There were other turning points in his collecting career: for example, when he was put in charge of the school cooker aged ten.

James has grown up to be a building surveyor. The front room of his house is now an oven showroom. He has eleven of them at home, with up to 200 in storage. Does he use different stoves for different dishes? 'Yes.' What's the appeal? 'Ovens from the 1930s to the 1950s were so nicely made. People get very nostalgic about them. I've seen people in tears when they lose the cooker.' James is well-known by the cooker manufacturers and he gets offered up to three each week. In fact this could be just the beginning, James has a website on the way, a large selection of utensils to go with his cookers and his dream is to have his own museum.

**"I've a cooker for sweets
and a cooker for savouries."**

FANATICAL CLOCK WATCHERS

You don't acquire the largest collection of cuckoo clocks in the world without being dedicated. Roman and his brother are committed to what they do – they spend every day of the year working to raise money to pursue their hobby. Even when they have time off, they use it to enjoy another collection they've got – vintage motorcyles. 'We don't really have a family now. We eat, live and sleep what we do. Even till 10pm on Christmas Day...'

And it's not just any old cuckoo clock they collect: it has to be constructed within a 25 mile radius of the Black Forest in Germany. The pair go on frequent trips to town halls and archives there to seek out rare examples, and their clocks are the envy of the German National Museum. Cuckooland, the museum that they run, has 566 antique cuckoo clocks including trumpeter clocks, which play a fanfare, and monks singing the angelus. Roman is fascinated by the craftsmanship. The museum is open to groups and, as you would expect, when the hour strikes, there is a tremendous racket.

**"It's like a jigsaw puzzle –
there is always that one piece missing."**

SEEING SOMETHING IN A GRAIN OF SAND

Dave was happy to look at sand under a microscope and dabble in geology. Whenever he visited an unusual beach he liked to pick some up. Then one day he typed 'sand collectors' into an internet search engine. It was the beginning of something big – he became part of a worldwide community.

'I soon got requests from all over the world to send sand samples. The universal unit of exchange would fill a 35mm film canister,' says Dave, who now finds he has to decline a lot of the requests.

His friends and family also fetch samples from their holidays, although they are not all familiar with the universal unit of exchange and bring back supermarket bags full of the stuff. For Dave collecting is about the love of hoarding things and the search for the unattainable. He catalogues all his samples and lists them on his own website. Do you meet up with other sand collectors? 'Certainly not.'

"It's an interest that got a bit out of proportion."

THE VIRTUAL MUSEUM CURATOR

The internet has changed the world for collectors. It makes it far easier to find people who share your interest, simpler to photograph and display your collection, and, if you log on to the auction site Ebay.com, you can acquire almost anything. Website manager, Jeremy, knows this well.

His Virtual Valve Museum is at www.tubecollector.org. It began with a precocious interest in electronics, and he now has 1,000 valves in the attic. He can wax lyrical about the WW2 Cavity Magnetron, which was the first valve to make radar really work, and was then used in microwave ovens. Valves appeal because 'it was the era of electronics when you could see things work.'

Another nice thing is to physically possess the valves, rather than just looking at them in books. His grandfather used to show him inside old radios, and indeed it is the 'antique wireless scene' that provides Jeremy with opportunities to trade and swap his valves.

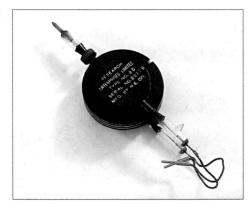

"It is a select hobby."

STILL PLAYING SPACE INVADERS

Five years ago Jim read an article about arcade games and decided that he wanted one. They were far too expensive. Using his skills as a silversmith and jeweller, he decided to build his own. 'I like collecting them as wrecks. I spend more time fixing and repairing them than playing them.'

Although Jim tries to interest the younger generation in his arcade games, they tend not to be impressed. 'Today's Playstations are much more advanced. They see these as relics, with no interest at all.'

But Jim defends them. He's got six in his spare room. He sees the early games like the early cinema – Robotron and Battlezone were produced by the early masters and demand 'classic game play'. Arcade game collectors, it appears, like nothing better than to get together, drink beer and play video games at weekends in someone else's garage.

"I like getting the games I played as a kid."

RULING PASSIONS

The slide rule was the main tool used by engineers and scientists for calculation until the 1970s. Since the invention of the pocket calculator, it has disappeared from use. Ron is 'the exception to the rule', as it were.

He has a slide rule website which receives 1,000 hits a day. He corresponds by email with aficionados from Ecuador, Zimbabwe and Australia. He stores his collection of 250 under the bed in the spare room. 'I take interest in the objects I collect,' says Ron. 'I regularly spend time with my slide rules.'

Slide rules were first developed in the 1620s. Artisans would use them to calculate things like the number of planks you could get out of a log. There is even an international club with 400 members called the Oughtred Society (www.oughtred.org) and a British one which goes by the name of the UK Slide Rule Circle (www.sliderules.org.uk). Ron and his friends meet to reflect on the historical development of the rule. What does Ron's wife think? 'She's not scientific, but she tries to get me a slide rule for Christmas or birthday.'

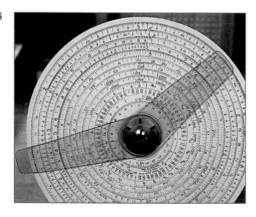

"I have rules for sewage flow, spring design, sugar pricing, electronics and structural design."

THE SUCROLOGIST

Talking to Roger you realise we first had the sugar cube, then the sachet, and now we have the tube. Roger has a network of 40 agents bringing him unusual sugar packets from all over the world. He and his wife regularly have to give up their weekends to sort the things out. The collection amounts to about 6,000.

How much history can be contained in a sugar wrapper! Roger has several from Laker Airlines, others from the General Post Office, and many from hotels that have gone bust. From America, he can see that sugar is going out of fashion: they've gone over to Candarel.

Roger empties the contents and mounts them like stamps. 'I could have filled a truck with the sugar. Unfortunately there is not a single person in my extended family who still takes sugar in their tea. The only use we have for it is to make custard,' says Roger, who considers many of his sachets to be small works of art.

"I wouldn't say there is one in every town."

SIGNPOSTS TO THE PAST

Traffic Warden John has about 100 road signs and 70 railway signs. They adorn the utility room, the hall, the bedrooms, the toilet, the kitchen and the landing. 'The wife doesn't mind them when they're displayed like paintings. It's when I leave them leaning on the skirting board there's trouble. I also tend to stub my toe on them in the middle of the night,' he explains.

The cast iron railway signs are his favourites. They can cost anything from £100 to £2,500. They remind him of a more solid time, when they didn't make them out of plastic and tin. 'Once you get one or two, themes come into it, and you start collecting sets. The people who collect railway memorabilia are a small, close-knit community,' he adds.

All John's signs are acquired legitimately at auctions and junk shops. 'If any go missing in the local area the police come round and look in my garden.'

LANCASHIRE & YORKSHIRE
RAILWAY
PUBLIC NOTICE

ALL PERSONS ARE HEREBY WARNED NOT TO TRESPASS ON THIS RAILWAY OR ON ANY STATION OR OTHER WORKS LANDS OR PROPERTY OF THE LANCS & YORKS RAILWAY Co

EVERY PERSON SO TRESPASSING AFTER THIS WARNING WILL BE PROSECUTED AND WILL BE LIABLE UNDER SECTION 36 OF THE LANCS & YORKS RAILWAY ACT 1884 TO A PENALTY NOT EXCEEDING FORTY SHILLINGS

BY ORDER

HERBERT MORRIS, LTD.
•EMPRESS WORKS LOUGHBOROUGH.•
LOAD 20 CWTS.

"Many signs are recyled as nails."

81

THE MAGIC OF MEMORABILIA

Bob's father used to talk about the circus. Young Bob developed a fascination with magic. One day in the late '60s he acquired a toy magician in the shape of a moneybox – somehow it linked the circus with magic and started a craze.

For 20-odd years, Bob was an export sales manager for a biscuit company. He saw a lot of the world, but it also allowed him to pick up bits and pieces of circus memorabilia: jigsaws, board games, posters, programmes, ornaments, clockwork novelty toys. They now bedeck his house.

'My wife is equally interested, which is good,' says Bob, who is now retired. He goes to circus events in Monte Carlo and Paris every year, and he tours the antiques fairs and car boot sales in England. 'It gets you out of the house, particularly in winter when you can't go in the garden.'

"Many wives don't allow their husbands to show their collections."

GETTING IT OFF YOUR CHEST

Des was once a badge entrepreneur. In the 1970s he went along to a concert hall, where a friend of a friend had a stall selling handmade puppets. It wasn't working, so he offered to take the stall and sell badges. He did so well that the management asked him to leave.

This gave him the confidence to set up his own badge shop instead, and he enjoyed the 'badge boom' of the late 70s. After that faded away, Des began amassing his own collection. He specializes in 'button badges' and has about 8,000. His best ones date back to the Boer War; he's also fond of the 'laminated screen bridge' ones (like the 3D postcards). He particularly liked those with slogans: 'I used to be indecisive – but I'm not so sure now' was one.

Des now goes round the country promoting environmental causes. Badges don't obsess him in the way they once did, but he's still a member of the Badge Collector's Circle (www.badgecollectorscircle.co.uk).

"I don't wear badges any more."

85

CANNY ART

An artist, designer and writer, Simon has given lots of thought to his collection. 'It's an ironic collection – after all you can't get many things more commonplace than a baked bean tin,' he says. Simon began by collecting tins for the practical purpose of storing his pens, brushes and crayons. But the urge to specialize in baked beans took over.

He is fascinated by packaging and graphics, so he decided to make a collage of his best bean tins and frame them on a piece of linoleum he found on a skip. He explains, 'I call it "Doubt and Certainty". There is something certain and immutable about beans. The labels are the same, with their pictures and brands, but then again there are very dissimilar things about them.' For a while, Simon would open his cans from the bottom so they looked untouched. However, the completion of Simon's work of art seems to have satisfied his longing to collect them. Did you actually eat the beans? 'Oh yeah, definitely.'

"I have made an aesthetic work out of my collection."

A COLLECTOR IS NOT ALWAYS LOYAL

Many collectors are devoted to more than one collection. David used to collect postboxes and also convert beautiful inlaid sewing machine cases into mailboxes. Then he realised how attractive the sewing machines were, themselves.

He has a passion for the machines that date from 1860 to 1901. He joined a Sewing Machine Club in London and acquired them from Germany, America and Canada. He has 200 of the things which he exhibits to the public in a barn converted to a museum. Is it popular? 'Oh yes.'

The postboxes are in there as well. Many of the sewing machines he has restored, his wife also uses a couple from time to time. A former clerk of works in the building trade, he admires the engineering and the workmanship of the old ones. 'The artwork is terrific: lilies of the valley, birds and flowers.' David also collects tobacco jars…

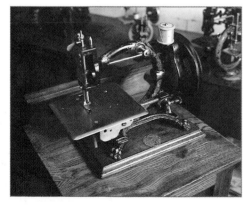

"They never wear out."

A WISE GNOME

Ron is special among collectors because he has actually become part of his own collection. He offered to grow a beard for charity and it stuck with him. Twice a week now he puts on his gnome costume and goes to his local market to collect money for good causes.

A retired window cleaner, Ron started collecting gnomes 40 years ago. He even has rubber moulds to make his own. 'Girlfriends love it,' he says. Though gnomes are not universally loved, it seems: the Chelsea Flower Show will have nothing to do with them. However, one Christmas, Selfridges, the London store, visited Ron's house to get inspiration for their window display.

'When I get dressed up as a gnome, I go into fantasy land,' says Ron. He gets stick from some people, but children see nothing unusual about him being 'Mr Gnome'. They regularly come to talk to him about his collection and are particularly solicitous of his welfare.

"You never find a miserable gnome."

MEMENTO MORI

Perhaps because Steve is fascinated by things that are buried in the ground, he is acutely aware of his own mortality. 'When I pass on, I'd like to leave the information I've collected to the county I collected it in.'

Steve remembers the first fossil he found, which he still has: an 80 million year-old sea urchin. A childhood interest became a passion after he got married. He spends weekends and spare hours curating his fossils, storing them in a stable environment and collecting data on card indexes.

He doesn't buy any; he finds them. But the equipment needed to clean them up is very expensive. Steve specialises in one stratum, but he won't reveal which stratum it is.

Steve has no academic training; he enjoys the unique approach he brings to the subject. He gives lectures and does his own research, when he is not being a heating and plumbing installer.

"At the end of the day,
you can't take them with you."

ACKNOWLEDGEMENTS

The interviewing skills used in the making of this book were honed on the many unusual characters of Paddington immortalised at www.newspad.co.uk. The author would like to thank Guy Browning, a collector and generous supporter of unconventional people who pursue eccentric projects.

For help with research, thanks go to the following individuals and organisations: Ann Atkin (The Gnome Reserve); Hannah Blake; Dr David Bradford; Stephen Cooper; John Dent; Wyn Dollicker; Len Ede; Andreas Gammel; Mark Gatehouse; The Gnomes of Gnymet; Jim Goedert (The Barbed Wire Collector); Sam Hallas; Robert Hazelby; Neal Herd; Bageshwar Jha (Sulabh International Museum of Toilets); Frank James; Derek Jones; Susan Jones; Stephen Kenneth; Raphe Langdon; Charlotte Lee (Duck Planet); Gareth Leighton; Steve Ludlow; Roger Mabbutt; Alan Marshall; Rex Morton; Richie Naylor; Neil Ramsden; Arthur Reeder; Pete Roberts; Colin Robbins; Jacky Smith; Fons Vanden Berghen; David White (Concept Websites Ltd).

All the collectors featured can be contacted through the publishers. Yasha Beresiner can be contacted at InterCol, Camden Passage, Islington, London 020 7354 2599.

First published in 2003 by
New Holland Publishers (UK) Ltd
London • Cape Town • Sydney • Auckland
www.newhollandpublishers.com

Garfield House
86-88 Edgware Road
London W2 2EA
United Kingdom

80 McKenzie Street
Cape Town 8001
South Africa

Level 1, Unit 4
Suite 411, 14 Aquatic Drive
Frenchs Forest,NSW 2086
Australia

218 Lake Road
Northcote, Auckland
New Zealand

10 9 8 7 6 5 4 3 2 1

ISBN 1 84330 554 2

Editor: Gareth Jones
Editorial Direction: Rosemary Wilkinson
Designer: Paul Wright
Photographers: John Baxter, Laura Forrester

Reproduction by Modern Age Repro House Ltd,
Hong Kong
Printed and bound by Craft Print International
Pte Ltd, Singapore.

PHOTOGRAPHIC CREDITS

John Baxter: Cover – Back (Middle-Top,
Bottom); pp 10–11; 16–17; 22–23; 26–27;
30–31; 34–35; 40–43; 56–57; 60–61; 68–79;
82–83; 90–91; 96.

Laura Forrester: Cover – Front, Back (Top,
Middle-Bottom), Spine; pp 2–9 12–15; 18–21;
24–25; 28–29; 32–33; 36–39; 44–55; 58–59;
62–67; 80–81; 84–89; 92–93.